The new tie

Series editor: Keith Gaines

Illustrated by Nina O'Connell

Nelson

"I'm going to a party today,"
said Jip.
"I need a new tie.
I'll go to the shops and buy one.

Will you come with me, Ben?
You could help me to buy a new tie."

"All right," said Ben.

"Which shop shall we go to?" said Ben.

"We must go to a shop that sells good ties," said Jip.

"What about this one?
There are lots of ties in the window."

They went into the shop.

"Can I help you?"
said the man in the shop.

"Yes, please," said Jip.
"I want to buy a new tie."

"I've got lots of ties,"
said the man.
"I'll go and get them."

He went to get the ties.

"Here you are," said the man.
"Have a look at them."

"Can I help you?"
he said to Meg.

"Look at that one," said Ben.
"It's got spots on it.
Why don't you try it on, Jip?"

"All right," said Jip.

He put the tie round his neck.

"No," he said.
"I don't think I want
a tie with spots on it."

"Look at that one," said Ben.
"It's grey like me.
Try it on, Jip."

"All right," said Jip.

He put the tie round his neck.

"No," he said.
"I don't think I want a grey tie."

"Look at that one," said Ben.
"It's got flowers on it.
You would look lovely in that tie, Jip.
Why don't you try it on?"

"No, Ben," said Jip.
"I don't want a tie with flowers on it.
I would look very silly in that tie.
I won't try it on."

"Well," said Ben.
"You have looked at lots of ties, Jip.
You don't like any of them.
You will have to go to
the party in your old tie."

"No, I won't," said Jip.
"I've seen the tie I want.
It will be just right for me.
I'm going to try it on."